THE REMNANTS *of* GOD

BETH BIDWELL

ISBN 979-8-89243-756-1 (paperback)
ISBN 979-8-89243-757-8 (digital)

Christian Faith Publishing
832 Park Avenue
Meadville, PA 16335
www.christianfaithpublishing.com

Printed in the United States of America

Contents

A Glimpse

In the beginning was the Word and the Word was with God and the Word was God. At Uasin Gishu town in the beautiful country of Kenya, a baby came forth. Born to his parents, James and Julia, they named their son Geofrey Nyaga. The family relocated from Eldoret to Nyandarua County after the Independence in the '60s.

He underwent his primary education at Uhuru Primary School, then later moved to Nakuru Town for his secondary education. He went to church and was baptized, then confirmed as a full member of the church. He became a youth leader very active in missions. While in the second year of high school, he surrendered his life to Jesus Christ and enjoyed being saved. He became a church school teacher at a church. Dr. Arthur Children's Ministry was one of his passions in the various areas of service in the church.

In the search for daily bread, he began tailoring a skill he learned from his dad. He designed school uniforms which he later sold in big markets before school opened. In Kenyan culture, kids attend school with a uniform, so Geofrey's business did good. He made enough money for his basic needs which were good for a high school graduate. He was able to buy a camera that he used for his second job as a photographer. In those days, in the '80s, he would take photos, then after a few days, he would deliver them to the people. For many years, he did photography as a job until he got into full-time ministry.

Later, he was employed as a church evangelist by the larger Church Nakuru Parish. During his off days, he did farming. He leased a piece of land, and he planted various crops mostly maize for extra income. He kept on believing in God and serving Him with total devotion.

His call to ministry was what led him to join the Church Pastoral Institute Kikuyu in 1988. This was a dream come true since he encountered Jesus Christ in his second year of high school. The fire in him kept burning. What a blessing to pursue his calling. In 1989, he graduated and was sent to Chogoria Presbytery for a two-month externship. Later he was posted to Pwani Presbytery Church, St. Margaret Parish.

He married his fiancée in 1990, a wedding so colorful. The kids he taught at the church school performed a song they had composed for the couple. It was a surprise yet so memorable. His wife supported him through his ministry and moved with him to all the churches till his last church. They were blessed with two daughters, all glory and honor to God Almighty.

Geofrey's practicals took about a year, then he was licensed and ordained in 1991. Reverend Nyaga served in various Parishes till his last breath. For thirty-three years, he served as clergy in the Lord's vineyard, walking humbly with God.

1992–1994 Dundori Parish 18 Churches
1995–2001 Kerugoya Outreach
2002–2003 Mathaithi Parish
2003–2008 Kahawa West Parish
2008–2010 Makadara Parish
2010–2014 Ngemwa Parish
2014–2016 Kiunyu Parish
2016 Sep–2017 Jan Gatundu Parish
2017 Oct–2021 Umoja Presbyterian Church

Further Studies

Clinical Pastoral Education (CPE) 2002 at Lay Training Centre & Kikuyu Hospital

Course on Drug and Substance Abuse for Trainer of Trainers 2003 at Lay Training Centre

HIV/AIDS Education in 2006

Diploma in Christian Ministries 2008–2010 at Nairobi Evangelical Graduate School of Theology (NEGST)

Bachelor of Ministry 2011–2013 at Andersonville Theological Seminary GA

Earthly awards and academic achievements are okay, yet all this is vanity if you don't have a relationship with God. Declare with your mouth that Jesus Christ is Lord and believe in your heart that God raised Him from the dead, and you will be saved. And so it is, "Whoever believes and is baptized will be saved but whoever does not believe will be condemned" (Mark 16:16).

Overcoming Adversities

Many are challenges people face in this world. What really matters is how to cope so that you can overcome. Reverend Nyaga encountered hardships in the ministry, and the Lord rescued him. In the daunting moments, the Holy Scriptures made him wise.

Reading the Bible and praying daily was a culture in his house. Knowing that all scripture is God-breathed so that the servant of God may be thoroughly equipped for every good work. Reverend Nyaga made the Bible his reference. He was dependent on God to fight his battle, so he put on the full armor of God for him to stand against the devil's schemes.

One day, a guy faced Reverend Nyaga and said, "You have touched the untouchables." It was in a meeting after the reverend asked the whereabouts of the money after fundraising was done. Some people said it was not deposited in the group's account, and the guy got defensive and threatened the reverend. A few weeks later, a letter was delivered at Reverend Nyaga's house. It was very awkward, unlike other mail via the box. From the look on his face, anyone could sense discomfort. It was a death threat addressed to him. By this time, Reverend Nyaga was hosting a student minister who he had been training for over two and a half months. The student minister who was American asked to read the letter, and her response was, "Are there human carnivores in this area?"

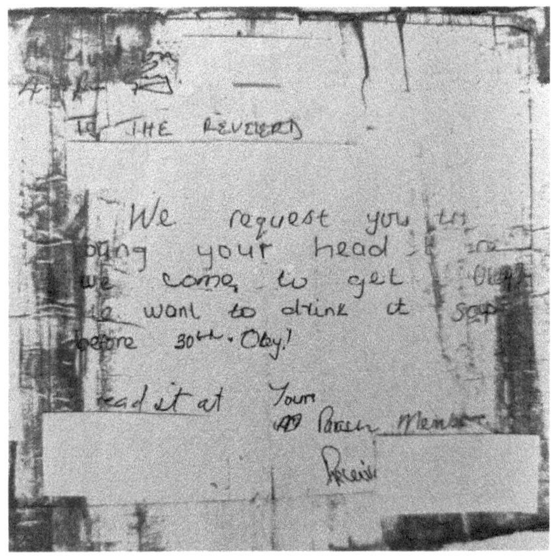

Reverend Nyaga said a prayer, and then we started heading to the car and drove off to a safe place. Just like there was a plot to kill Jesus Christ after He raised Lazarus from the dead, now it was a plot over the reverend. Encouraged by the words from John 15:3, I have told you these things so that in me you may have peace. In this world, you will have trouble, but take heart! I have overcome the world. He knew that finding a safe place was vital to save his life, his family, and the guest American student minister for the night.

The issue was reported to the police, and they provided protection until our guest booked an earlier flight and was ready to leave. If you read John 11:45–57, you see that Jesus Christ no longer moved about publicly among the people of Judea, "But the chief Priest and the Pharisees had given orders that anyone who found about where Jesus was should report it so that they might arrest him."

Persecutions, sufferings, then enduring
for the crown of righteousness

That was such an ordeal to experience, and surely God saved us. When Reverend Nyaga got into ministry, he was aware there would be affliction. The reality came when he experienced so different from the Bible stories he had read. Through all this, God's faithfulness was proven to us. With His mighty hand, He protected us.

His biggest lesson was some battles you don't have to fight physically. If it's time to run, just go because God will watch over you. The day to take the student minister to the airport came, and off we all drove to Nairobi. Unfortunately, we were late, and the plane left. We found a motel, and then the next day, we headed to the airport. Sorrowful as we bid goodbye because she was such an amazing buddy.

She said, "I keep praying for you that God may watch over you." Off she went. What a relief!

Shall we ever see her again? Happy and sad at the same time. Happy that she was safe heading to her home in Atlanta. Sad because we enjoyed her company and the good times we had like visiting Lake Nakuru National Park, but all in all God had protected us through it all.

What shall we say to these things? If the Lord had not been on our side, when men rose up against us, they would have swallowed us alive when their anger flared against us. Reverand Nyaga told his family. By faith, God will open a way for us to go to the USA and meet her. As time went by, she kept in touch for some years by mail to the new town that the reverend moved to.

That trying time did not pull him down rather he persevered for he knew, greater is He who is in him than who is in the world. The Lord gave him the strength to keep on reaching out to the lost. The words from 1 Thessalonians 5:16–18, "Always be joyful. Keep on praying no matter what happens, always be thankful, for this is God's will for you who belong to Christ Jesus," were such an encouragement to his soul and his family.

In the midst of serving, he encountered yet another struggle. His health was challenged, and after going to the doctor, he was said to have a lifelong condition. He said, "I still put my faith in God. He will never let me down in the middle of this thorn. I will overcome. For when I am weak, then I am strong because of Christ Jesus."

At that time, he was working and not getting paid. Catering basic needs and other bills became a challenge. The story from 1 Kings 17 became a similar reality. Like Elijah being fed by the ravens during the drought season became so real in our family. God stirred up generosity in some people who visited the reverend's house with loads of groceries that lasted a long time, and we never lacked food. One was a youth who made sure to care for the servant of God in his town. A few years later, God opened a way for him to work in a foreign country, all glory and honor to God our Provider.

The other was a group of three ladies from a former church where the reverend had ministered. On the very day they visited on a Saturday afternoon, it was when the reverend had received a call from his daughter, saying, "Dad, I have been sent away from school due to school fees balance. I will be getting at home in the afternoon."

He told her, "Alright, my dear, just come home. God will provide, and you will be back to school soon."

By the time the daughter came, the guests were chatting with the reverend, and his wife was preparing a meal.

One of the guests asked, "What are you doing at home? Shouldn't you be at school?"

As a child so innocent, "There was a school fees balance, so they sent all who hadn't cleared home."

There was a pin-drop silence, and the lady looked at the reverend and said, "Tomorrow in the afternoon, please meet me at a certain parking lot, and I will be having the amount needed for your daughter to go back to school."

The joy was evident on the reverend's face, and the family was in awe of the goodness of God. It was a joyous moment everyone held hands, and Reverand Nyaga prayed a blessing upon the wonderful ladies who had been sent by God. True to her word, the next day, the family met with the lady. She had an envelope with the money for school, and she had doubled for the reverend as a token.

She said, "The Lord who brought us to your house had a reason."

A few years later, she and her husband bought land and built a mansion, and she invited Reverand Nyaga to officiate the housewarming.

Even in the dry season, God visited the family of Reverend Nyaga, for they tasted His goodness. Like we say the God of Elijah, in this case, the God of Reverend Nyaga, the miracle-working God provided. In Genesis 18:1–15, Abraham and Sarah's hospitality to the three visitors made them receive a son the following year. In Kenya and the African community, hospitality is a practice for a guest whether they have called before or not.

One day after the service, Reverend Nyaga walked home, and it began raining heavily. He had to cross a creek, and due to heavy rain, the water level had risen, and he struggled to crossover. He almost drowned, but he held on to a tree branch that was floating, and he was able to swim to the other side despite the overwhelming flood. Indeed God saved his life as He promised in Isaiah 43:2, "When you pass through the waters, I will be with you, when you pass through the rivers, they will not sweep over you." At the season, Reverend Nyaga was serving eighteen churches.

Through the rejection, mockery, and being looked down on, Reverend Nyaga never backed down from preaching to Word of God. He was able to keep his head above the water and never was Reverend Nyaga ashamed of telling the world about His Savior Jesus Christ. All glory to God for strengthening Him throughout His life. He preached to fulfill the purpose of Him who called him into ministry. One great personality Reverend Nyaga had, and what we admire is the smile he kept on his face even when he was among his opposers/mockers.

There were times when situations got unpleasant, and his back was against the wall. Reverend Nyaga fixed his eyes on Jesus Christ. He leaned on God to help him every day because he couldn't handle life alone. He read and preached about the beatitudes from Matthew 5:11–12, "Blessed are you when people insult you, persecute you, and falsely say all kind of evil against you because of me. Rejoice and be glad because great is your reward in heaven for in the same way they persecuted the prophets who were before you."

When you're going through trials, remember that your worth is defined by God, so never stop believing in Him. Therefore, be still and know that He is God, and nothing is too hard for Him. When God shines his light on you, you will rejoice so never abandon God.

Public humiliation is something that happened to Reverand Nyaga, and by God's grace, he handled it well. Like King David's soldiers were bitter in spirit after the Amalekites took their families, and they wanted to stone him. Acts of atrocity were done to the reverend. At that moment, he felt like he would curse them, but he remembered that verse in Matthew 5:44, "But I tell you, love your enemies and pray for those who persecute you." He chose to show kindness to his oppressors because he knew that God will fight for him.

> No weapon formed against you shall prosper, and every tongue which rises against you in judgment you shall condemn. This is the heritage of the servants of the Lord and their righteousness is from me, says the Lord.

Reverend Nyaga endured so much more than can be written. One thing that was definite in his heart, he would overcome because of Jesus Christ then his victory was guaranteed.

In this life, as we journey to heaven, we will face hardships, the distinction will be how we handle it. Giving up should not be an option. Believe that you are a conquerer through Christ Jesus, and you will make it.

> Do not be afraid of those who kill the body but cannot kill the soul. Rather be afraid of the One who can destroy both soul and body in hell. (Matthew 10:28)

> Don't let my enemies laugh at me; they hate me for no reason. Do not let them make fun of me, they have no cause to hate me. (Psalms 35:19)

> May those who want to take my life be put to shame and confusion, may those who say to me "Aha! Aha!" turn back because of their shame. (Psalms 70:1–3)

All this is written in the Bible so that we read of their experiences and get encouraged when we are on this journey. To persevere and know that God is with us.

The Good Times

Count your blessings name them one by one and see what the Lord has done in your life. How can we find the best words to express our gratitude to God in the journey of Reverend Nyaga? There are more than thousands of reasons to thank God for His goodness.

In a certain church, there was a group of youth that decided to show kindness to their reverend. They organized a fundraising and from the money they collected, they bought Reverend Nyaga a vehicle. Inspired by the commitment, Reverend Nyaga had to serve God no matter the distance between the eighteen churches he served since they financially supported his ministry. Such an awestruck moment for Reverend Nyaga and his family. The God of wonders had come through from riding a bicycle to driving a car. Praise be to the name of the Lord! Blessed are them all who supported his ministry. Till the time of Reverend Nyaga's demise, he remained friends with them.

Another part of Ministry that Reverend Nyaga enjoyed doing was Crusades and conventions/conferences. Some would run for a week or four days depending on the organization. This was an epoch-making time for soul-winning. Door-to-door missions during the day and in the evening open-air preaching at the center of the marketplace. In Kenya, open-air preaching is known as crusades, which is commonly done.

During this time, there would be guest preachers and gospel musicians from all over the country who were Ministering. All the guests were being hosted at Reverend Nyaga's residence. They ate and drank there because the Church had organized certain women to prepare meals. One thing Reverend Nyaga taught his children from an early time was sharing coz the kids had to give up their beds for the guests. It became a norm, and they quickly adopted it because it was annual.

He called out people to salvation at the end of the preaching and prayed for the sick and others who came forth with needs. Caring for the flock of God was the most important way so that Christ may be magnified.

Reverend Nyaga was an outgoing, jovial person who would associate with all without discrimination. At the shopping centers, he would chat with the alcoholics/drunkards whom nobody else wanted to come close to for they were dirty from falling into muddy puddles or barely taking a shower. They could recognize Reverend Nyaga from afar because most of the time he wore his clerical collar. In a certain parish, he organized an event for the alcoholics where he shared a meal with them and shared the Word of God with them. Not ashamed or afraid to share the Good News of Jesus Christ, he would tell them, "God loves you. He sent His Son Jesus Christ to die for your sin so that you may be saved please let Him into your life to change you for the better." He prayed with them and laid his hand on them at the shopping centers. People who were around would even come out of their shops to stare at Reverend Nyaga while he was praying. Like Jesus was a friend to sinners and how they got inspired to follow him wholeheartedly so was Reverend Nyaga doing reaching out to the lost. Praise the Lord, most of them gained salvation and spread out the light.

Reverend Nyaga a down-to-earth servant of God usually gave his phone number out to the congregation before he started the Sermon. He said, "I want to give you all my number. Feel free to call me anytime night and day if you need prayers. This was a controversy to some and because they didn't like that, they tried to make things harder for the reverend.

"Remember that there is one you can call unto always, his name is Jesus Christ, and He will help you," Reverend Nyaga said.

During his time in the ministry, he received many calls from members. Some he prayed for and others he took action. Two great instances where he helped different couples to go to the hospital at night because their babies were almost being delivered, luckily they got to the hospital before, all thanks to God. Many times at night he received calls from members who wanted to be taken to the hospital cause their family member was critically ill.

Without hesitation, Reverend Nyaga used his car to serve God by helping the needy people. After getting back home, he would clean his car with a smile on his face though he was cleaning the mess. He taught his family being kind, humble, meek, and merciful is vital in life. There was an instance he offered to help a family to transport their dead relative to the mortuary. He lowered the back seats so that the person's body was able to fit, and Reverend Nyaga drove to the mortuary. He found joy in helping, whether morally or spiritually, Reverend Nyaga found opportunities to make a difference in the world and did it wholeheartedly. He would give people a lift some of whom walked over two kilometers to get to church or to the bus stop. Even if he got in his car with muddy shoes or had luggage, he never complained.

He said, "My car is also for serving the community around me if they need help, all for God's sake."

There came a group of seven to Reverend Nyaga's residence. They came to check on their pastor. To fellowship with him and his family, they bought him a microwave, which is not a common appliance for most people in that country. To their surprise, they found him lying on the couch because he was sick. He had been unwell for a few days but was not so critical to go to hospital. One of the guests was a nurse, and she decided to check on him.

Reverend Nyaga was treated with an IV which she had to go get from the hospital and for a week she treated him daily till he was well. These people became prayer warriors for the ministry of Reverend Nyaga. They understand that the weapons of our warfare are not carnal but mighty through God to pull down strongholds. These wonderful visitors said to Reverend Nyaga, "We are here to support you like Aaron and Hur did for Moses." In Exodus 17:12–14, when Moses's hands grew tired, they took a stone and put it under him, and he sat on it. Aaron and Hur held his hands up, one on one side, one on the other so that his hands remained steady till sunset.

Delighted by the doing of God, Reverend Nyaga still prayed for the guest before the left. Surely the Lord was his banner, sending help to him at a time when he felt ill. All glory to God because Reverend Nyaga recovered and continued ministering.

Do you ever pray for your pastor or clergy from the church you attend?

Are you among the ones who want to stone the clergy instead of using the stone for support?

In various parishes where Reverend Nyaga ministered, there emerged groups of women who made it a priority to visit him and his family. They said that charity begins at home so we have to take care of our pastor. Youth groups too visited Reverend Nyaga, and he was grateful to see their commitment to serving by caring for their clergy. One of the unforgettable moments was when some youths decided to volunteer to cultivate the farm where the reverend's manse was built. They later on shared a meal at his house, they were so comfortable around him, and it was epic. In the very little things, he was marveled by the goodness of God.

On a Sunday afternoon, a youth group decided to surprise Reverend Nyaga and his family. He was left speechless by their good deeds. They brought furniture for the living room and dining room as he had moved to a new house. He was thrilled by the way they were used by the Lord to become a blessing to his family. All Glory to God for it is not by might nor power but by the Spirit of God.

There came a time in the reverend's life when things seemed hopeless in human eyes yet God poured out his mercy. In distress, Reverend Nyaga called on the Lord, and God sent a good Samaritan. Full of empathy, the good Samaritan hosted Reverend Nyaga for over five months. With a roof over his head, he ate and drank with no pay. When it seemed as if it was over, God made a way. This was a miracle he never forgot till the day he took his last breath. The pain and shame were taken away, God beautified his life.

Another breathtaking moment in Reverend Nyaga's ministry was when a group of youth visited him. They planned to visit him in advance so they had a meal prepared for them. Over fifteen people from Kirimara were in the house, and they all had a blast. They had a preacher, and after the sermon, they had gifts for Reverend Nyaga and his family. Remarkably they had bought outfits for Reverend

Nyaga, his wife, and his daughters. Tears of joy flowed down his face as he worshipped God, and everyone sang along such an incredible fellowship. God is good all the time, forever may He be praised. Reverend Nyaga got an opportunity to preach at the radio station called Kameme early mornings for a few months. He was hosted by the late Njoki Ndegwa who was a member of the Church Reverend ministered.

Reverend Nyaga had the privilege to be a leader in the fellowship of Interdenominational Clergy's in the town of Kerugoya.

He also became a member of the priesthood fellowship which consists of clergy from different denominations here in the Pacific Northwest.

He enjoyed preaching in schools primary and secondary for their morning devotions. At some high schools which were boarding schools, he would have a service on Sunday and give Holy Communion. He also participated in the end-of-the-year exams prayer day which was being conducted for children who were going into high school or clearing their high school education.

Reverend also organized trips for church members some were farming and others were site visiting.

While in Kenya, it's tradition that police have stop checks so when they would stop him, he would gladly greet them and tell them about Jesus Christ because he was unashamed.

Another part of the ministry he enjoyed was visiting each member's home for prayers. It happened with their availability, and Reverend Nyaga went to visit and pray together with his wife. Reaching out to all because they were all important.

great!

ARIA YOUTH FELLOWSHIP

Church Planting

Reverend Nyaga's zeal for evangelism was evident. He pioneered several church planting in Kenya. One of the ways that he enjoyed was the door-to-door missions. Reverend Nyaga and his team also organized the open-air preaching the the towns where the church was to be started. His greatest accomplishment was winning souls for the kingdom of God, thus making more disciples to spread the good news.

In some places, people walked over an hour to church, so opening a Church close by was vital.

1. Church Malindi
2. Church Mukinduri
3. Church Kahara

> He said to them, "Go into all the world and preach the gospel to all creation Whoever believes and is baptized will be saved but whoever does not believe will be condemned." (Mark 16:15-16)

He did this wholeheartedly for God not to be recognized in their history. For to whom much is given, much is expected. He mentored different people who were in the various churches he ministered. They thrived in preaching the Word of God and are now witnesses in different towns. Some were in the same denomination, and others planted their churches.

They are Pastor Baba Bachia, Pastor Mama Eli, Pastor Baba Ndau, Rev. Dr. Gitare, Baba Shem, Baba Brian, Baba Ngobia, Pastor Virginia and Mama Dodo.

ALL NATIONS
PRESBYTERIAN
Church
Matthew 28
WELCOME

The Transition

Moving to various towns was something that Reverend Nyaga and his family were accustomed to. This time, the move was different from one country to another, one continent to another. God of Reverend Nyaga visited him in a great way, he had been selected as a winner in the Green Card Lottery.

Filled with excitement after getting the news, he held hands with his family in a thanksgiving prayer. Surely God's love never fails, and His promises are yes and amen. Reverend Nyaga had been playing the lottery for quite some time, and at God's appointed time, all things worked together for his good.

Every time he played the lottery, he would say, "God will open a way, and I will win." He prophesied to himself and believed God was capable of doing it. Reverend Nyaga really liked this verse in Hebrews 10:35, "So do not throw away your confidence, it will be richly rewarded." By faith, Reverend Nyaga was located in God's favor.

In such a short time of serving Gatundu Parish, they were kind enough to organize a farewell party for Reverend Nyaga and his family. It was such a memorable moment that Reverend Nyaga never forgot. Their kindness and generosity to their clergy were spectacular.

When God wants to bless you, He does not consult any man. If it were so, some people would be stumbling blocks giving out reasons why you shouldn't be blessed. Being a well-known clergy, Reverend Nyaga had to inform his friends, and there was another farewell party in a different town. All glory to God for his faithfulness.

In the midst of celebrating the blessing, Reverend Nyaga encountered discouragements. A few who said, "Pastor, at your age, why should you be going to another country? How are you going to cope with finding another career when you are almost retiring? You should really think about it. You don't have to go."

Reverend Nyaga responded with a smile, "God did this miracle, and who am I to say no to the GREAT I AM?" "God provides for His own. I trust that He will show us the way. If He did it for the Israelites, He will lead us by His pillar of cloud by day and pillar of fire by night. What is unknown to us is known to Him so we will continue trusting Him."

Finally, the d-day came for Reverend Nyaga and his wife to fly to USA. They were exuberant for the next chapter of their life for Ebenezar had blessed them. At the airport, his family and a group of ten-plus members of Church Gatundu waited to bid them farewell. They sang and prayed to magnify God for his loving kindness.

Reverend Nyaga said, "We waited patiently for God, and now we are experiencing his faithfulness. What we prayed for has come to pass ooh! See what the Lord has done. After a word of prayer, Reverend Nyaga and his wife checked in, and off they flew to Boston. God showed his eminence and presence in Reverend Nyaga's life, so that it may be known all over the world that there is nothing too hard for God, to experience Him, you need to have faith.

Reverend Nyaga frequently said, "Serving God is not in vain." They arrived in Boston and were received by his brother and a few friends. Jubilation as they reunited all the glory to God. Reverend Nyaga was hosted by his brother until he moved to Washington.

Along his journey, he came across people who told him, "Reverend Nyaga, you can start your own church. You don't have to be working under an organization. It's much better managing your personal church."

He responded to them, "You know, I have heard your perspective, but I choose to wait and see what God has installed for me." Reverend Nyaga chose to follow his God what had always led him, putting aside other voices.

Reverend Nyaga never compromised his loyalty to his God. Being a follower of Jesus Christ was his mission. Just perhaps they never understood he acknowledged the Church is the Bride of Christ. Reverend Nyaga was unshakable in his belief for he had seen the goodness of God. He never wanted to do what others were doing though they seemed to be succeeding.

Reverend Nyaga said yes to the will of God, where the Lord led him, and he followed. He surrendered to God, whenever the moment God chose, whatever God's plan for him, he was ready. All that matters is that the will of God was done in him. Humble he was and his soul said yes to God's will.

By the grace of God, they were able to get by the culture shock and the winter. As for everyone in an unfamiliar culture it tends to get challenging and by the grace of God, you come out victorious. One of the things he had to adjust was driving. For over twenty years of driving on the left in Kenya, he had to learn to drive on the right. The other was the winter season, experiencing snow for the first time was interesting, and he took lots of pictures for that.

He was welcomed by some of the Kenyan those whom he knew and those he didn't. God made a way for Reverend Nyaga, and he was invited to Preach in some of the Kenyan-based churches in Boston, Delaware, Missouri, and Washington. During the week, he worked in the health department, and on the weekends, he was a church minister. Nearly four years he worked as the reverend of Umoja Presbyterian Church P.C.U.S.A.

Serving under the P.C.U.S.A was a great experience after he had served the church. He learned the difference in the liturgy and was able to adjust. The most important thing for him was serving and worshipping ONE GOD.

On the verge of being homeless, Reverend Nyaga and his wife got a miracle. A good Samaritan offered to stay with them. The good Samaritan hosted them for over six months in his house without paying any bill. It was a miracle after they encountered a hardship that left them with the choice of either going back to Boston or being homeless in the streets of Washington. In the midst of that the Almighty God provided because he is Jehovah Jireh, He never leaves us or forsake us. The good Samaritan is a person of a different race, yet one who knows Jesus Christ and with the fruit of the Holy Spirit called love offered to help until they were financially able to rent their apartment.

One thing he never changed about his personality was humility. He was a humble and ever-smiling guy, I bet anyone who met him would attest to that. A man filled with the fruits of the Holy Spirit was Reverend Nyaga. Twice he went to Kenya, unfortunately, for the burial ceremony of his relatives. He got the opportunity to meet some of his friends who were awesome.

They said, "Reverend Nyaga, you look so good. You have changed a lot."

He would tell them, "It is God's doing, Ni Mwathani. Yet not I but through Christ in me."

God lifted him from one glory to another. The goodness and mercy of God followed Reverend Nyaga all the days of his life as he dwelled in the house of the Lord. He would often say I would rather be a doorkeeper in the house of my God than dwell in the tents of the wicked. Reverend Nyaga got an opportunity to Preach in New Jersey and enjoyed fellowship with brethren at Pilgrim Presbyterian Church who were Church Partners since he was in Kenya. His last sermon was at Umoja Presbyterian Church Washington before his demise on Monday.

Sermons

Here are a few of all the sermons he had given for the past thirty-plus years in ministry.

Theme: Wait

In reference to Isaiah 40:31, "But those who wait upon the Lord, shall renew their strength they shall mount up with wings like eagles, they shall run and not be weary, they will walk and not be faint."

In the waiting, be joyful and develop an attitude of gratitude. Instead of grumbling, worship sing out and declare, "I know my God is able, and He will beautify my life. Rejoice in the Lord always. Ignore negativity around you and fix your eyes upon the Lord. The vital thing is to keep reading the Word of God and pray fervently daily.

David waited for a long time after he was anointed till when he was made a king. He got many opportunities to kill Saul, but he didn't. He believed his time would come, so he waited and never got weary even after being chased by Saul.

Hannah waited and prayed without ceasing. God gifted her with Samuel, and she kept her promise, and then God enabled her to get five more children.

Don't be impatient. Wait on God.

We cannot go without you

Many are times when we have to make some changes in our lives. Whether moving to a new house, town, job, or any other venture of life. Stepping out of the comfort zone can be challenging,

and we need to know that with God all things are possible. He is the
GREAT I AM, He did it before, and He can do it again.

Isaiah 45:1–5 and Psalms 5:8:

> I will go before your and will level the
> mountains, I will break down gates of bronze and
> cut through bars of Iron.

He is a dependable God, a promise Keeper so relax because you
are in good hands.

> I will give you hidden treasures, riches
> stored in secret places, so that you may know that
> I am the Lord the God of Israel, who summons
> you by name.

Oh my! What a joy divine to know that God knows you by
name, and all He says He will do for you. Love is so amazing from
your Creator. He says He will bestow on you a title of honor

May your soul be uplifted and know that He is the Lord, and
there is no other apart from Him.

Theme: something sweet "ngogoyo"

> The righteous will flourish like a palm tree,
> they will grow like a cedar of Lebanon. (Psalms
> 92:12)

Doing what is right in accordance with God will make you
flourish. As the palm trees stay deep-rooted and green withstanding
the weather so can you withstand all the temptations. Jesus did it, so
you can.

Reverend Nyaga gave an example of the cedar fence at his parents' home. The fence was from the late '60s, and until now it's hold-
ing up.

Imagine how much better it is to be growing in our relationship with God and remain faithful, "Planted in the house of the Lord, they will flourish in the courts of our God. They will still bear fruit in old age they will stay fresh and green"

How good it is if we continue bearing fruits even in old age. Being kind, gentle, loving, empathetic, and also telling people about your Jesus.

Every chance you tell to the world without hesitation of how God is the best, greatest, and most reliant God among the other gods who are the works of men. He gave His Son Jesus Christ to save us. The only solid rock to stand on because all other ground is sinking sand

May you be the source of something sweet and change the world positively by living life in a manner worthy of the Gospel of Christ.

The Remnant-Matigari

> Even so then at this present time also there
> is a remnant according to the Election of grace.
> (Romans 11:5)

> Except the Lord of hosts had left us a very
> small remnant, we should have been like Sodom
> and we should have been like Gomorrah. (Isaiah
> 1:9)

This word *Remnant* in Kikuyu language "Matigari" became something Reverend Nyaga emphasized a lot mostly during the corona period from 2020 till his demise in June 2021. He said, "I am a remnant, and you are a remnant too, God has let us see this day so don't take it for granted."

Repent, forgive those who have wronged you, keep on praying. God will save his people from the epidemic because human impossibilities are God's possibilities.

Reverend Nyaga overcame COVID-19 after a week of quarantine, he was zealous to express how Jehovah Rapha restored his health a moment he got nearer to God. Psalms 18:5 says, "The cords of the grave coiled around me, the snares of death confronted me."

Therefore, may you all remember to thank God for preserving your life and delivering you from the evil. God is a restorer. God is the one who made Shadrach, Meshach, and Abednego as the fourth man walking in the fire will also be with you, and His Remnants.

His last sermon: theme, loving God

Readings: Psalms 59:1-17 Luke 15:11-31

His prayer. Our king who lives forever, the unchangeable God, Lord our hope, our joy, our refuge and our strength we are waiting upon you, talk to us dear Father in a special way, teach us, let your Holy Spirit penetrate in our life so that we may do your will and your name may be Glorified and everybody will go home with joy, help us to know you and to come back to you.

Testimony. We have seen the presence of God walk with us this far. Christ Jesus today is my Lord and Savior, a faithful and trust-worthy God.

Call to worship. Jeremiah 32:18 says, "You show loving kindness to thousands but bring the punishment for the parents sins into the laps of their children after them. Great and mighty God whose name is the Lord Almighty."

Loving God and enduring in His presence is what we should do.

What a great love and peace that comes within.

We should maintain that love, extend God's love to others so that we are able to practice His will in this life

God will go before you despite your enemies trying to hurt you. He will cover you with His wings. He will ensure that you will never perish.

When you love God, you are able to serve others for the Lord's sake.

1. We must be *imitators* of God. "Kwihanania na Ngai" devoting yourself to the Lord.

    Being able to inspire and motivate others to following Christ. You should be identified as a child of God.

    The prodigal son left and misused all his inheritance, but when he came back to his senses, he was able to identify himself with his father. No matter how life had taken a toll on him, he knew his father would take him back.

    His father filled with love and compassion, ran and embraced him. God is ready to receive us when we repent.

    The Father's spirit and the Son's spirit were connected.

    Jesus Christ is our role model. We should resemble our Savior by loving others without discrimination.

    Are you ready to devote your life to God? Jesus sacrificed his life so that we could be received into God's kingdom.

    We shouldn't be like the other son who choose to discriminate/hate/envy while the father was celebrating the come back of his lost son.

    If we imitate Jesus Christ, we shall have a forgiving heart for anyone who has wounded us Jesus said, "Father, forgive them, for they do not know what they are doing." And they divided up his clothes by casting lots (Luke 23:34).

2. Do not be self-centered but look out for others.

    "Do not do things out of selfish ambitions or conceit but in humility consider others better than yourself" (Philippians 2:3–5).

    David said, "God will let me look in triumph on my enemies. Kill them not, lest my people forget." He was in pain and tried to be nice to his enemies by asking God not to kill them.

    Your attitude should be like that of Jesus doing all things with a clean heart.

"And being found in human form, he humbled himself by becoming obedient to the point of death even death on a cross" (Philippians 2:8).

May the Lord help us as we end this month to yearn to be Christlike, humbling and devoting our life to God.

Matthew 25:34–40

Attending to the needs of others like how the good Samaritan took care of the beaten stranger who was left half dead. He paid the cost for God's sake. Very empathetic he was.

For I was hungry and you gave me something to eat, I was thirsty and you gave me something to drink, I was a stranger and you invited me in. I needed clothes, and you clothed me. I was sick, and you looked after me. I was in prison, and you came to visit me. This question will be asked when we come face-to-face with God

May God help us so that we will be able to answer *yes* to this question.

Journey to a distant country

Going our own way and rebelling against God and his standards, shutting our ears from his words of direction is the wrong decision.

The Bible is the GPS that gives us direction to walk in God's path.

Following God's path steadfastly

When someone hardens their heart and doesn't want to be corrected, they are running away from God's love. They become selfish, rejecting God, and then they are uncovered, thus prone to danger.

In Luke 15:20–21, we see a reunion that teaches us of God's compassion and love when we repent and devote our lives to Him.

The son said to him, "Father, I have sinned against heaven and against you. I am no longer worthy to be called your son."

Remember God loves you, and He insists that you may spread his love to others.

Where are you my dear loved brother and sister in your relationship with your Creator, your God? Can you be identified as a child of God? In the name of the Father, the Son, and the Holy Spirit.

Call to salvation

> Here I am! I stand at the door and knock. If anyone hears my voice and opens the door, I will come in and eat with that person and they will me. (Revelation 3:20)

Jesus Christ is gentle and friendly. He does not want you to go through life alone. His love for you is to be led by His Father.

Please let him in your life, and He will never leave you nor forsake you.

> Jesus answered, "I am the way and the truth and the life. No one comes to the Father except through me. (John 14:6)

Surrender all to God. Repent for He is faithful. Don't lean on your own understanding.

God fixes our inner being and fills us with peace, joy, love, forgiveness, humility, and so much more.

Talk to God in prayer. Ask Him to create in you a clean heart so that you may worship Him in truth and spirit.

> Come to me all you who are weary and burdened and I will give you rest. Take my yoke upon you and learn from me, for I am gentle and humble in heart and you will find rest for your souls. For my yoke is easy and my burden is light. (Matthew 11:28–30)

Have you been struggling and have an emptiness that seems to never end? Come to Jesus Christ. He will satisfy you and fill you with peace. You are the one he came to save.

What a joy divine to live life with Jesus Christ as your everything. Your Savior loves you. Let Him lead you, for He will never lead you astray. Put God first, and You will flourish. Life without Jesus Christ is all in vain.

Then hold on to what you have so that no one will take your crown because Jesus Christ is coming soon. Always be ready. May Christ Jesus be magnified in you.

Whoever has ears, let them hear what the Spirit says to the Churches.

Traveled Home

Reverend Geofrey Nyaga was a traveler all his life. The most important decision he made was to have Christ Jesus in him, and then he never traveled alone.

One Monday afternoon, one of the extremely hottest days in the summer of 2021, Reverend Nyaga was found unconscious on the landing of the stairs at the apartment he lived in. His wife found him, and she called for help, and their next-door neighbor came to help her with CPR before the ambulance medics resuscitated him. Rev. Nyaga took his last breath.

The heat wave was shattering Tacoma, and it was 108 degrees.

The Lord took him home, the time had come, and no one could stop it. Reverend Nyaga's work on earth was over, and he left for paradise to rejoice with his Creator, the wonderful God whom he worked for.

Then what can we say, he fought a good fight and finished his race. Second Timothy 4:7–8 says, "I have fought the good fight. I have finished the race. I have kept the faith. Now there is in store for me the crown of righteousness which the Lord the righteous Judge will award to me on that day and not only to me but also all who have longed for his appearing."

Less than an hour after Reverend Nyaga's heart stopped beating, there was a flood of people coming to see if it was true. Lots of Kenyan's came to confirm if what they heard about the reverend was real. It was terrible to have a big crowd in a small space and the hot air. Once the house was opened, there were grocery bags and two packs of twenty-four water bottles by the door.

This meant he had just brought them in and was heading to the car to get another load. There were over thirty-five people in the house, and the water Reverend Nyaga had bought was given to them.

For the next weeks, prayers were held in the church where he had ministered for years.

Later on, Reverend Nyaga's body was flown to Kenya, his homeland, approximately a fifteen- to seventeen-hour flight. Exactly a month from when he went to be with the Lord, then was his burial ceremony. With three memorial services, one in Tacoma and two in different towns in Kenya was a hero celebrated. The unforgettable man of God, the ever-smiling reverend till his last breath. A crowd of seven hundred people attended his burial to pay respect to a faithful servant of God.

TO THE GLORY OF GOD
THIS MANSE WAS DEDICATED BY
REV. GEOFFREY G. NYAGA
MODERATOR OF
PRESE
ON
BLESSED ARE THOSE WHO DWELL IN YOUR
THEY ARE EVER PRAISING YOU
PSALM 84:4

A Tribute Was Not Enough
for a Legend

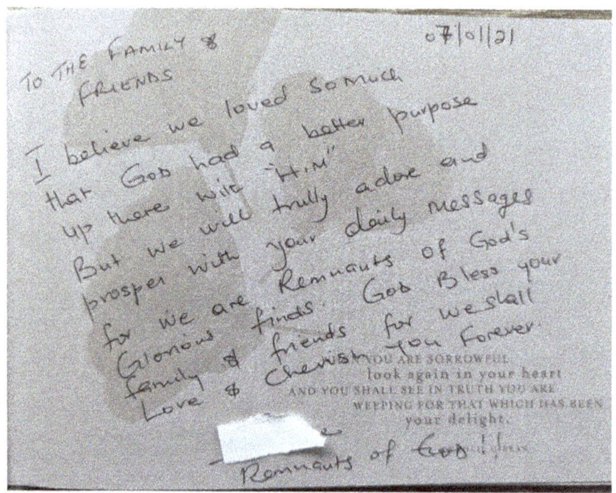

It was written by a friend on the Condolences book and
it says a lot about my Dad's sermons and the book

A tribute during his memorial service or the day he was buried could not be enough to describe who he was. The impact of his ministry in the church is unforgettable. Most of those who read a tribute never had full insight into how he became his authentic self.

At home, he was a dad and husband to his wife. At church, he was Reverend Nyaga or "Mutungatirii" in Kikuyu language. With the very short time, there was for the tribute. I could never say enough. The tribute wasn't for him, it was about him. He couldn't hear lying in a casket if I started expressing how I loved him, what good would it have been, so hypocritical if I had never told him while he was still breathing? Thank God I always reminded him that he is special and loved. I have seen people make that mistake and so I urge everyone to let your loved ones know you love them then you can't feel awful.

Reverend Nyaga kept telling his family, "You guys need to write a book and tell the world." Well, here it is now. Letting the world know his story, and surely his legacy lives on. Thanks to God Almighty.

Telling it as it is, a traveler whose destination was heaven, and no ranging storms would make him abandon his calling. The story of his life. God the Lifter of Reverend Nyaga's head faithfully fulfilled his promise like he said in Jeremiah 33:3, "Call to me and I will answer you and tell you great and unsearchable things you don't know."

Reverend Nyaga had his family's support throughout his ministry. His wife left the job to serve God together, and eventually, they did a music video together. A great father and grandfather he was.

Anyone who ever met Reverend Nyaga would attest that he always wore his cross pendant necklace. Unwavering about his faith in God and despite the ridicule from most of the people, Reverend Nyaga represented God to the fullest. His life was wholly bound to Jesus Christ. A better word to describe him. A man of people of God.

Your experience/story is important. If it were not so, the stories in the Bible would not have been written for generations to read and see God's majesty.

Reverend Nyaga persevered to teach people that the way to everlasting life is through Jesus Christ the only way, the truth, and the life. He wore his ephod because he believed God would help him overcome just like God helped David when he wore the ephod and won against the Amalekites.

Reverend Nyaga humbled himself, and he cleaned up trash from the church for the years he served. It came as a surprise even to the guests who visited the church while they saw the reverend collect trash. He made sure that the church was clean before he left because he was the last to lock the church. A down-to-earth servant of God just like Jesus Christ washed the disciples' feet.

Reverend Nyaga was blessed with the opportunity to host church partners from New Jersey. They traveled to Kenya to help in the church he served. He hosted them for the few days they came for missions. They became family friends, and when he relocated to USA, he visited them in New Jersey. A reunion so marvelous spending the weekend together. Reverend Nyaga was a man of faith, and His God fulfilled the promises He told unto him.

May the Lord help you do good and may His will be done in your life.

I hope you choose to support the servants of God sent to your church. Never be one of the religious opposers. Remember God called them into ministry.

Choose support instead of stoning.

> Now all has been heard, here is the conclusion of the matter: Fear God and keep his commandments for this is the duty of all mankind. (Ecclesiastes 12:13)

Acknowledgment

I would like to extend my most sincere gratitude to God Almighty for His steadfast love.

To my dad, Reverend Nyaga, for compiling most of this book, so I just did the finishing. May he enjoy his eternal life he always preached about.

To my mother, Nancy, for her tireless dedication in supporting Dad in the ministry, always welcoming and cooking for guests who visited the house no matter what time, very early or very late. For also composing a song and video producing it together with Dad. To my sister, Mercy, thank you.

To Rev.Dr J. Nyaga and his wife Mrs.Rev J. Nyaga for hosting my parents in the East Coast since their arrival in USA to when they moved to the West Coast.

To Reverend Wallace and his wife for being the most amazing spiritual parents for Reverend Nyaga.

To the family of both Reverend Nyaga and Nancy for their support throughout his ministry.

To Edith's family for attending to Reverend Nyaga health while he was in Kenya.

To the good Samaritan for your kindness.

To the Warutere's hosting Reverend Nyaga's wedding dinner party.

To the Church Kerugoya for supporting Reverend Nyaga and family when he lost his mother.

To Mr. Kariuki for baking a birthday cake for the family without requiring any payment.

To the people of God who supported Reverend Nyaga and his family in all the churches he ministered.

To the Kenyans in Seattle, Boston, and other states for your generosity after his demise.

To the youths in the USA church who surprised Reverend Nyaga by furnishing his house.

To the brethren in Kerugoya town for supporting the man of God during his time of service.

To the wonderful family friends who always hosted our family for vacation for a week in the Kenyan Coast Mombasa. For providing housing, food, and their one car for us to tour around while they went to work. Blessing upon them. The Kongos.

To the youths in Nakuru towns for buying Reverend Geofrey his first car after seeing him serve in over eighteen churches with his bicycle.

To the brethren in Kahawa West for their love and generosity.

To all brothers and sisters in Christ Jesus for having played a part in supporting Reverend Nyaga in his ministry.

Blessings overflow.

To the Olympia Presbytery of P.C.U.S.A for their kindness and guidance to Reverend Nyaga when he joined their team to be a clergy of one of their churches.

About the Author

Beth Bidwell is a Christian music minister. She is a Born-Again woman who writes music and has produced songs. She sings at church and anywhere that God sends her. She is a follower of Jesus Christ, and she believes in God the Father, Jesus Christ His Son, and the Holy Spirit. Bidwell grew up in Kenya and now living in the USA. She was brought up by Christian parents since her dad was a clergy, and her mother is a gospel music minister and ordained pastor. She has been serving God for the last seven years as an adult by choice.

Bidwell has an associate's degree from KTTC (Kenya) in information studies. By God's grace, she has read the Bible from Genesis to Revelation, and she continually reads it daily. She is a dental assistant by profession.

She believes that God calls the ones who seem unqualified from a human perspective so as to show His greatness.

She is called according to God's purpose to fulfill His will, following His ways every day. She goes to church because it is the house of her Father, and she knows there is and will always be a place for her. Bidwell's relationship with God and Creator comes first before anything or anyone.

She loves and supports people who have been hurt by religious leaders/followers because she has in the past experienced hurt and discrimination. Telling them that, in the house of God, everyone is welcome as they are, when they hear of Jesus Christ and then receive Him, He molds them to be like Him obeying God.

Bidwell's hope and prayer is to continue to reach out to many people and tell them about Jesus Christ. The way to enjoy life fully is to Matthew 6:33, "Seek first the Kingdom of God and His righteousness and the rest shall be added unto you."

Bidwell knows that life without Jesus Christ is in vain.